THE DESTRUCTION OF
POMPEII

MIKE ROSEN

Illustrated by
MARTIN SALISBURY

The Bookwright Press
New York · 1988

Great Disasters

Titles in the series:
The Destruction of Pompeii
The Sinking of the Titanic

Titles to come:
The San Francisco Earthquake
The Space Shuttle Disaster

First published in the
United States in 1988 by
The Bookwright Press
387 Park Avenue South
New York, NY 10016

First published in 1987 by
Wayland (Publishers) Limited
61 Western Road, Hove
East Sussex BN3 1JD

ISBN 0-531-18159-6
Library of Congress Catalog Card Number: 87- 71742

Phototypeset by Direct Image, Hove, E. Sussex
Printed in Italy by G. Canale & C.S.p.A., Turin

Front cover: *Pompeii AD 79; people run for their lives as Vesuvius erupts.*

Words that are printed **bold** the first time they appear in the text are explained in the glossary.

CONTENTS

A NARROW ESCAPE

The eruption of the volcano Vesuvius in AD79 killed thousands of people. This story reconstructs the events as they might have been seen through the eyes of a young boy.

"It was just before lunch. We were in the garden playing tag. My sister Lucilia had almost caught me when the ground shook so hard that we both fell over. Then the loudest explosion I have ever heard sent us running indoors. Our mother was in the **atrium**, her face pale with fear.

" 'What's happening?' I cried.

" 'It's an earthquake, Gaius,' replied my mother, 'like the one that destroyed Pompeii when I was young.'

"At that moment we heard a sound like falling hail. We looked up at the roof. Stones were falling through the opening meant for collecting rainwater. Some were at least as large as a man's fist. They rattled down the roof tiles and bounced on the floor next to us. I picked one up but dropped it quickly because it was burning hot. Just then Sabina, our cook, rushed in shouting: 'It's not an earthquake. It's Vesuvius. The mountain is on fire!'

"The ground shook violently again, so we huddled by the **lararium,** our family shrine, and waited in fear.

"Shortly, Eros, the **slave** who kept our father's business accounts, staggered in from the street. His head was bleeding. Breathing hard, he said, 'My master, Lucius Crassus, says I must bring you to the harbor. He has a ship there that will take us to Surrentum.'

" 'We cannot just leave,' protested my mother. 'Thieves will loot the house when we are gone.'

" 'You must leave before Pompeii is destroyed,' interrupted Eros.

" 'But the harbor is over a mile from here . . . ' mother continued. Then she changed her mind. She led us to the front entrance and stepped out into the street.

"Outside, the morning was growing dark. A dust cloud hung over the city, shutting out the sunlight. It cast a shadow on the slopes of Vesuvius, where fierce fires raged in the vineyards. We stumbled down the streets toward the harbor, keeping in the shelter of the houses. I tripped several times. The air was thick with fumes, which made it hard to breathe. My throat and lungs were sore and my eyes were streaming tears. Stones were still raining down so we clutched our heavy, woolen cloaks tightly around our heads to protect ourselves. A fine gray

Sabina rushed in from the street shouting, "Vesuvius is on fire!"

ash settled on the ground and burned our feet.

" 'Come in and take shelter,' called Calpurnia Lepida as we passed her door. 'Wait till the stones stop falling. You will be safe in here.'

"As if to prove her right, the ground shook and an avalanche of roof tiles crashed into the street behind us.

" 'But we must get to the harbor,' I urged. 'Father will be waiting.'

"We struggled on. Everywhere people were running wildly, crying and shouting. Some were rushing to the forum. Most were trying to get home. Outside the Temple of Isis there was a jostling mass of slaves and **freedmen** fighting to get in. They were shouting to the priests, 'Let us in. Let the goddess Isis protect us from the wrath of Vesuvius.' But we had no time for prayers, instead we rushed on.

"At the harbor all was noise and confusion. Our father embraced us, relieved to see us all safe. We hurried aboard ship, taking shelter from the falling cinders. The waves were wild and the wind blew hard, but we escaped the harbor safely. Behind Pompeii the flames from Vesuvius flared orange and yellow, spreading an ugly glow through the thick cloud of dust that was suffocating the city. I didn't realize then that this would be the last time that I would see the beautiful city where I was brought up."

Through the panic and confusion, Gaius and his family rushed down the streets of Pompeii to the harbor: "Stones were raining down and the ash choked our throats. We clutched our cloaks around our heads."

LIFE IN POMPEII

For most of its early history Pompeii was not a Roman town. The oldest buildings at Pompeii date from c.550BC, but little is known about the original, native settlement. Roman rule was imposed almost 500 years later. At first, Pompeians did not have Roman citizenship. This meant that Pompeians had to obey laws made in Rome but had no part in making them. It was not until 80BC that Roman citizenship was granted. At the same time, a large colony of retired Roman **legionaries** was set up at Pompeii. These two events brought Pompeii into a new era.

From its modest original settlement, Pompeii grew into an important city.

Pompeii was a trading town. Its position at the mouth of the Sarno River enabled it to control both **imports** and **exports**. After 80BC many rich Romans built villas along the coast and on the slopes of Vesuvius. Their wealth supported a local industry in luxury goods — jewelry, perfume and precious metal items. By AD79 Pompeii was a prosperous **commercial** center with an industrious, artistic and ever-increasing population.

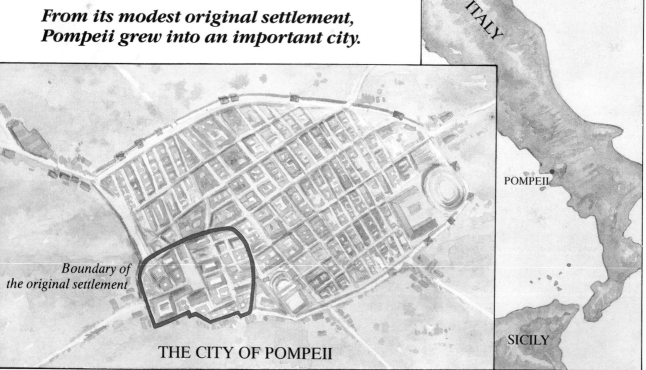

Boundary of the original settlement

THE CITY OF POMPEII

ITALY

POMPEII

SICILY

The forum, the city's chief meeting place and market.

Landmarks of the city

Pompeii's prosperity was shown in its impressive public buildings, concentrated around the forum. The forum was the center for business dealings and religious ceremonies. It bustled with activity all day. Stalls were set up along the covered passageways. Customers haggled fiercely over the price of a trader's goods, while in the covered markets for fish and meat, buyers fought to get the best bargains.

At the south end of the forum were the council offices and the basilica — the law court. The north end was dominated by the Temple of Jupiter and there were other temples along both sides. Pompeii's most powerful group of traders, the **fullers**, had their own meeting place in the forum — the Building of Eumachia.

Outside the forum, Pompeii's public buildings included an **amphitheater**, three bath-houses, a theater and a concert hall. The Pompeians were supplied with fresh running water by a system of **aqueducts** and pipes, which brought the water from nearby hills into public fountains in the streets where everyone could use it.

Domestic life

Private houses in Pompeii had one especially interesting feature: over the atrium the roof sloped inward to the center, which was open to the sky. When it rained, the water ran down this roof toward the opening through which it fell into the **impluvium** then down into a **cistern** where it was stored. This was how Pompeians had collected and stored all their water before the aqueduct and public fountains were built.

Owing to Pompeii's growing population, many houses had extensions or upper floors that were added later. Only a rich family could

A Pompeian meal in a room decorated with wall paintings.

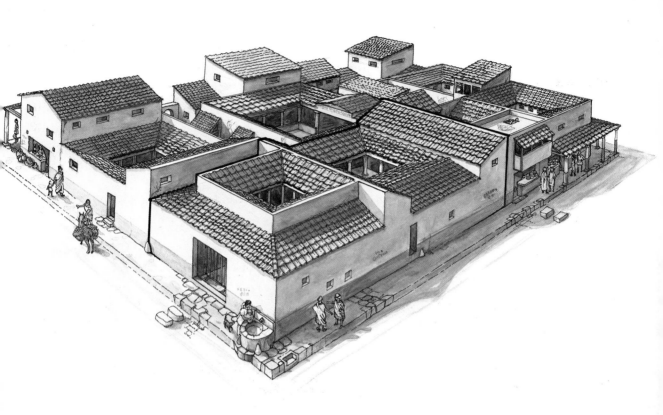

A Pompeian insula (block of houses). The house on the corner in the foreground, with its roof openings for atrium and garden, is typical of a wealthy Pompeian's home. At the corner of the street you can see a man drawing water from a public fountain.

afford a large house, so all the rooms in a house were often rented to different people. Sometimes whole families lived in one room. Rooms facing the street were rented as taverns or stores, and sometimes entire houses were turned into laundries, bakeries or perfume factories. In Pompeii, rich and poor, family and business lived and worked close together.

Pompeian families were controlled by the father. Women were unfortu- nately given very little independence under Roman law. Richer families owned slaves who carried out all the chores around the house. Sons of such families received some education at school, but girls were only taught what they needed to know in order to run a household. Poorer families had no slaves, and the children had to work for a living from an early age. Life at that time definitely favored men — rich men especially.

Pompeians at work

Pompeii's main industries produced wine and woolen cloth. For the latter the Pompeians used a process called **fulling**, which made new-woven woolen cloth ready for domestic use. Many Pompeians made a living by producing luxury items and by exporting and importing goods. For instance, Pompeii exported local agricultural produce, especially wine and olive oil, to as far away as North Africa and imported pottery made in the south of France. Slaves ran most of Pompeii's businesses on behalf of their owners. Such slaves were well-educated men, captured in foreign wars and kept for their knowledge and skills. If they served their masters well they might receive their freedom — and even the business.

Below *Milling flour, and three stages of fulling — washing, treading and weaving.*

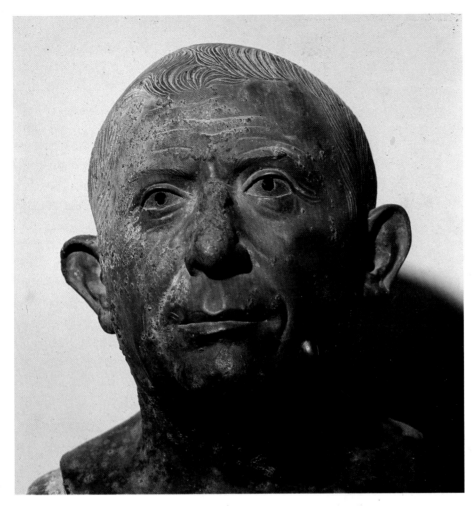

A bronze sculpture of the wealthy Pompeian banker Lucius Caecilius Jucundus. A large number of receipts were found in his house. These have told historians much about Pompeii's economy.

Politics

Many of Pompeii's richest men were freedmen, but although free, they were unable to vote or run for public office — only male citizens had those rights.

Whereas freedmen could have wealth but no direct political power, many citizens could vote but were poor. Freedmen often agreed to support a citizen as a candidate for election. They would pay for his campaign and in return the citizen would look after the freedman's interests while in office. Political campaigns could be very expensive because the votes of poor citizens were often bought by giving them free food. Once elected, politicians were expected to pay for public buildings such as the baths and the amphitheater and to put on free entertainments for the people. That was why only a wealthy person, or a citizen with rich backers, could afford to be elected.

Above *A* lararium. ***The figures represent the household gods.***

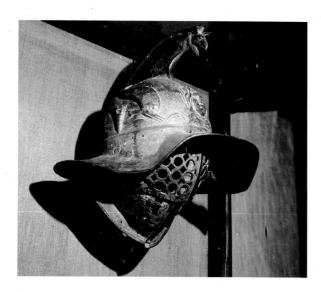

This helmet was probably worn by a gladiator in combat.

Religion

Politicians were also expected to present gifts to the city's gods and to repair the temples. To Pompeians the gods had all the vices and virtues of humans, but were more powerful. They would pray and offer gifts to keep the gods happy and Pompeii safe. If neglected, the gods would turn vengeful and bring disaster to the city. Gifts and prayers were also offered daily at a family's own *lararium*. These rituals honored both the gods and the family's ancestors. In times of danger people sought refuge in temples. Unfortunately these were to offer little protection against the effects of Vesuvius's eruption.

Rest and relaxation

If they wanted to relax after work, Pompeians had a wide choice of activities. A visit to the baths was one of the most popular. The Stabian Baths were the largest in Pompeii. Inside was an exercise area, a swimming pool and hot and cold baths.

The hot and cold baths were like a modern Turkish bath. After changing (men and women bathed separately), bathers spent some time getting used to heat in the *tepidarium* (warm room). Then they moved into the *caldarium* (hot room) where the floor was so hot the bathers had to wear wooden shoes. They sweated in the steamy heat for as long as they could. Next came a hot bath followed by a plunge in the *frigidarium* (cold pool) after which they were massaged with oils. Finally dirt and dead skin were scraped off with curved metal blades, which the Romans called strigils.

Pompeii also had two theaters, the larger of which could seat 5,000 people. It had awnings to provide shade in hot weather. Sometimes perfumed water was sprinkled on the audience. Sad to say, little has survived of the plays performed, because they were rarely written down.

Pompeii's amphitheater seated 20,000 people, who came from Pompeii and nearby towns to see the shows. **Gladiators** were the main entertainment. They were usually slaves or criminals, and were known by the type of weapons with which they fought. Most were killed on their first appearance, but if they survived for long and earned the respect of the crowd they could win wealth and freedom.

Rich men often paid for private performances of songs or poetry in their own homes. For poorer people, Pompeii had numerous taverns where they could drink, gamble and play games like checkers and dice. Like any modern city, Pompeii had something for all its inhabitants.

The **tepidarium** *(warm room) in a women's bath-house. The baths were very useful in a noisy and dirty city. Many Romans used the baths every day.*

VESUVIUS EXPLODES

Sometime between 11 a.m. and noon on August 24, AD79 the eruption started. With a massive explosion Vesuvius's solid crater split open. A cloud of **pumice stone** and dust spread across the sky. **Lava** ran down the slopes. Within minutes the pumice started to fall on Pompeii. The wind was blowing to the southeast, scattering ashes over a large area. Anyone who escaped Pompeii by road may well have died later in the countryside. Escape by boat would have been safer because the wind would have forced boats along to Surrentum — out of danger.

By the evening of the same day, Pompeii was over 6½ ft deep in stones and ash. Anyone taking shelter indoors was trapped, and some were crushed by collapsing roofs. Many bodies have been found buried under the ash. These people probably died by choking on the hot ash in the air or from the poisonous sulphur gas given

Below *The extent and depth of the ash fall. Note the route taken by the Roman admiral Pliny the Elder on August 24, AD79.*

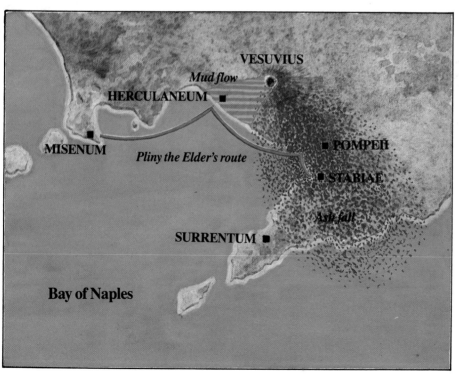

off by volcanic pumice and ash while cooling. This could rapidly make breathing indoors impossible. Even in the open air such fumes could kill babies, old people, and those with weak chests. It is also possible that a large volume of this poisonous gas, heavier than air, rolled down the slopes of Vesuvius. The inhabitants of a villa at Boscoreale, near Pompeii, appear to have died in this way.

On the morning of the next day, August 25, Vesuvius's crater walls

Burning pumice stones rained down on Pompeii.

collapsed inward. When a new series of explosions sent more dust and ashes into the sky, the dust cloud became so thick that no daylight could get through. Earthquakes caused tidal waves and damaged buildings around the Bay of Naples. Toward afternoon the wind began to blow to the west — bringing danger to new areas.

The rain of ash and cinders stopped

on August 26, but danger had not yet passed. Torrential rain fell on the ashes that lay thick on Vesuvius's slopes. On August 27 these ashes became a landslide of boiling mud, which buried the coastal town of Herculaneum. Few people died at Herculaneum itself, because many people fled before the landslide. But the latest excavations have found the remains of hundreds of people who were killed when seeking shelter on the seashore.

Above *Pliny the Elder, who died on the beach at Stabiae while trying to rescue a friend.*

How we know what happened

Much of our knowledge about the eruption comes from the excavations at Pompeii, and from the study of other volcanoes in action. There are also two letters written by Pliny the Younger, who was staying in Misenum, not far from Vesuvius, when it erupted.

Pliny tells how his uncle, Pliny the Elder, was naval commander at Misenum at the time. Three hours after the eruption started, Pliny the Elder set sail to investigate. An attempt to land near Herculaneum was unsuccessful because ash and rubble was already blocking the shore. Pliny the Elder did not attempt to land at Pompeii, instead he headed for Stabiae. There he found his friend Pomponianus ready to leave but unable to do so. The wind that

had favored Pliny's southward journey now trapped them at Stabiae. After a bath and dinner, Pliny retired to bed.

Toward morning on August 25, Pliny's friends awoke him. Ashes and stones were filling the courtyard outside his bedroom. He was in danger of being trapped. Earthquakes were shaking the building, and it was safer in the open. Pliny went down to the beach, but the rough seas and contrary wind still prevented escape. A little later, overcome by fumes, Pliny the Elder collapsed and died.

The change of wind in the afternoon of August 25 brought danger to Pliny the Younger, who had remained at Misenum. The dust cloud overtook him in open country:

". . . spreading over the earth like a flood . . . darkness came upon us. Not the darkness of a moonless or cloudy night, but as if the lamp had been put out in a sealed room. You could hear the shrieks of women, the wailing of infants, and the shouting of men . . . ashes fell on us. We rose from time to time and shook them off to avoid being crushed and buried by their weight."

Soon after the eruption had ended, survivors returned to Pompeii. Those parts of buildings that stood above the ash were taken apart for use elsewhere. Eventually nothing visible remained and soil covered the site. The memory of Pompeii lived on only in the name local people later gave the area — *Civitas,* or city.

Left *The baths at Herculaneum. Solidified volcanic mud blocks one of the doors.*

Right *Pompeii, looking south toward the forum; revealed after almost 1,800 years under ash.*

VOLCANOES

There are about 500 volcanoes in various parts of the world today. The earth's surface, or crust, is made up of a number of sections called plates. The place where two plates meet is called a fault line.

Beneath the plates, at depths of 2 to 35 miles (3 to 56 km), the rocks are liquid — melted by the heat from the earth's core — and contain bubbles of hot gases. The pressure of these gases increases the movement of the plates along the fault lines. Movement of the plates is normally very slow. Earthquakes result when they move suddenly. It is along the fault lines that most of the world's volcanoes are found. Vesuvius lies on such a line, along with Etna and Stromboli — nearby volcanoes. Only a few volcanoes are found in the middle of

Pressure in the magma chamber blows out the plug.

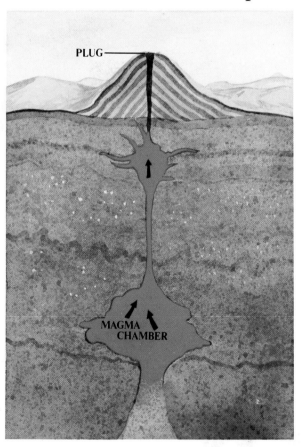

PLUG

MAGMA CHAMBER

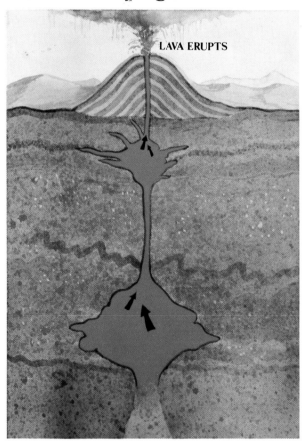

LAVA ERUPTS

Red-hot lava erupts from Mount Kilauea Iki, Hawaii.

plates, but wherever located they serve as an outlet for the powerful pressures within the earth.

Volcanoes can lie dormant for many centuries, depending on the activity beneath the plates. Before the eruption of AD79, Vesuvius had been inactive for almost 1,000 years. An eruption only occurs when the pressure beneath the plate becomes strong enough to force a hole in it or to force the **magma** through existing cracks. Along the fault line on which Vesuvius rests, one plate is being pushed under another. The result is that millions of tons of rock are being forced below the crust and turned into magma. With more magma under the plate, pressure increases. The pressure forces magma through weak spots in the crust. A volcano is just such a weak spot.

When the magma reaches the surface it may be free to flow out or it may be blocked. Mount Etna in Sicily is in a state of almost continuous eruption. Lava flows break out regularly from a number of different points on the slopes of Mount Etna. As a result, the pressure inside is released a little at a time. In contrast, the eruption of the volcano Vesuvius in AD79 showed the consequences of a blockage.

Left *The fiery beauty of a lava flow seen at night.*

Below *With Vesuvius now dormant, guides take tourists deep into its crater.*

When a volcano lies dormant, magma deposits in the crater and in the shaft leading up to it may cool and solidify. They form a plug, which prevents further, minor eruptions. If the magma cannot escape, the pressure builds up. Eventually the pressure becomes strong enough to blast the plug out. The plug is smashed into millions of fragments, the crater's sides often collapse inward and the explosion sends this vast cloud of dust and rock thousands of feet into the air. This is what happened at Pompeii in AD79. Today Vesuvius's shape retains traces of its original crater. Known as Mount Somma, it lies to the northeast of Vesuvius's present cone.

There have been some other extremely destructive eruptions and it is interesting to compare them with that of Vesuvius. On August 27, 1883 most of the island of Krakatoa disappeared. It was part of an enormous volcano. The eruption sent tidal waves crashing against neighboring islands — killing over 32,000 people. Ash from the explosion rose 50 miles (80 km) high and fell all over the world. The shock tremors were felt thousands of miles away at Alice Springs in Australia.

In 1980, the eruption of Mount St. Helens in the state of Washington released enormous dust clouds. Fortunately, Mount St. Helens was in a remote area and few people died, but the dust cloud drifted across the country, ruining crops. It also affected weather conditions around the world.

In 1980 Mount St. Helens in Washington erupted, producing huge dust clouds.

OTHER DISASTERS

Before the eruption of AD79, Pompeii suffered two other major disasters. In AD59 there was a serious riot in the amphitheater. The occasion was a gladiatorial show sponsored by a man called Livineius Regulus. Gladiators from Pompeii and the neighboring town of Nuceria were opponents in the contest. Spectators from both towns were present. Some small incident in the crowd led to taunts and abuse being hurled between Pompeians and Nucerians. Trouble flared as stones were thrown and swords were drawn. Fighting in the crowd upstaged the gladiators, who must have looked on in amazement.

When the fighting finally stopped, many Nucerians were dead or wounded. The Senate in Rome banned

Reliefs carved after the AD62 earthquake. **Above** *The Temple of Jupiter topples over,* **and below** *oxen escape from under a falling gate.*

gladiatorial shows at Pompeii for a period of ten years as punishment, and Livineius Regulus was exiled.

Even without gladiators, Pompeian life continued to be spiced with danger. Three years later, in February AD62 an earthquake caused severe damage to buildings. The city's water distribution center was affected, and flooding added to the problems. It is not known exactly how many people died. The earthquake may have been a warning that Vesuvius was becoming active again, but earthquakes were common in the area and few people would have seen it as a sign of greater destruction to come. Pompeii was slow to recover from this disaster. The forum was still under extensive reconstruction when Vesuvius erupted.

REDISCOVERY

The first discoveries at Pompeii were accidental. In 1534 and later in 1689, workmen digging canals found remains of Roman buildings. Coins and statues were removed but the discoverers did not realize they had found Pompeii.

Starting in 1748 the rulers of Naples — the **Bourbons** — sponsored various excavations at Pompeii. These were little more than attempts to plunder artistic treasures, although they did expose the buildings rather than just tunnel into them. Deep shafts were dug at Herculaneum, precious items were extracted and the shafts then filled in. Anything removed was taken to the Bourbons' private museum. By archaeological standards great damage was done by these excavations. But they did confirm the rediscovery of Pompeii.

From 1861 onward, the excavations began to be treated more seriously.

Left *Excavating Pompeii at the turn of the century. In the center of the photograph you can make out a painted wall that has been uncovered.*

Opposite, above *A plaster cast of a victim.* **Opposite, below** *Giuseppe Fiorelli making a plaster cast.*

Giuseppe Fiorelli was appointed chief archaeologist. Fiorelli introduced new archaeological methods. For instance, all finds were carefully noted in a journal and, as far as possible, they were left where found instead of being taken off the site. The location of the finds was precisely recorded on a plan also devised by Fiorelli. This plan divided Pompeii into numbered regions. Within each region the *insulae* — blocks of houses — were also numbered, as was each entrance to an *insula*. As a result of such methodical work it became possible to learn what buildings had been used for, and what sorts of people lived in them.

Fiorelli's most spectacular invention was the process of filling cavities in the ash with plaster. This produced detailed impressions of whatever had caused the cavity — usually bodies or wooden items that had long since decomposed. There are many plaster casts of victims of the eruption, showing the horror of their deaths. From one garden came a cast of a baby in its mother's arms.

The site at Pompeii today

The principles of archaeology that Fiorelli introduced inspired his successors. Amedeo Maiuri, in charge from 1924 to 1961, developed these principles further. He began to restore walls and ceilings in selected buildings. Ordinary domestic and business items were left in position. In this way visitors could get a glimpse of life in pre-eruption Pompeii. Today much of the site remains to be excavated. Archaeologists using modern equipment record and analyze discoveries.

A modern archaeologist studying ancient human remains.

Preservation experts work on mosaics and wall paintings to protect them from the weather. Wind, rain and recent earthquakes continue the destructive process started by Vesuvius. Preserving the ruins already uncovered is as vital as continuing the excavations.

A visit to the site today conveys the scale of the disaster. Crumbling buildings everywhere show the power of nature. The streets are roughly paved and deeply rutted. Grass and weeds grow up between paving stones, and run rampant through some of the excavated houses. In the early morning, there are few people around and Pompeii is an eerie ghost town. Later in the day, the streets are thronged with visitors who bring back some of the bustle that must have characterized Pompeii in AD79. In the site museum there are Pompeian statues and some of Fiorelli's plaster casts of victims. The impressive size of the public buildings emphasizes the Romans' building skills. Inside the private houses, paintings, mosaics and gardens reveal an artistic civilization. On a wet day, the rain runs down a restored roof into an *impluvium* just as it did 2,000 years ago. At such moments it is easy to imagine what it was like to have lived in the town Vesuvius destroyed.

Pompeii today. The streets are brought to life by visiting tourists.

FURTHER INFORMATION

Archaeology is about discovering the past. All around the world, human history is waiting to be discovered under the earth. Sites like Pompeii are rare, but there may be ruins near you from which you can learn a lot. Perhaps you might even be lucky enough to find another site like Pompeii! If you would like to visit a site or join a dig, you should be able to find out where to go at your local library. There may be a group of people in your town interested in local history who know of archaeological sites nearby. Museums with archaeological collections may also know where you can join excavations in progress.

If you ever travel to the south of Italy you can visit the excavations at Pompeii and Herculaneum. While there, you can climb or ride to the top of Vesuvius and go down into the crater. The National Archaeological Museum at Naples contains many of the most important statues and other finds from Pompeii. Museums around the world have collections of Roman objects. It's always worth visiting one to get a better idea of what the Romans were like.

BOOKS TO READ

Here are some other books you may find interesting. Most can be found through local libraries.

Lost Cities by Roy A. Gallant. Franklin Watts, 1985.

See Inside a Roman Town, rev. edition by Jonathan Rutland.
     Franklin Watts, 1986.

The Shadow of Vesuvius: Pompeii AD Seventy-Nine by Raleigh Trevelyan.
     Merrimack Publishing Circle, 1976.

Small World of Romans by Ivan Lapper. Franklin Watts, 1982.

Pompeii by Ian Andrews. Lerner Publications, 1980.

Pompeii: Exploring a Roman Ghost Town by Ron and Nancy Goor.
     Crowell Junior Books, 1986.

Pompeii Two Thousand Years Ago by A.C. Carpieci. Larousse Publishers.

GLOSSARY

AD Anno Domini — any year after the birth of Jesus Christ.

Amphitheater A building, usually circular or oval, in which tiers of seats rise from a central open arena where contests are held.

Aqueduct A channel used to carry water.

Atrium The main room of a house. The *lararium* and the family strongbox were kept here.

BC Before Christ — any year before the birth of Jesus Christ.

Basilica A law court. Also used as a meeting place for businessmen.

Bourbons Rulers of the state of Naples, 1734 to 1861, before Italy became one country.

Cistern A tank for storing water.

Colonnade A covered area where the roof is supported by a row of columns.

Commerce The buying and selling of goods and services.

Export To sell or transport goods to a foreign country.

Freedman/Freedwoman A man/woman who has been freed from slavery.

Fulling A process of treating new-woven woolen cloth with chemicals, then combing and stretching it. Once this is finished, the cloth can be made into clothes or other woolen goods.

Gladiator A slave who was forced to fight other slaves, as an entertainment for the public.

Impluvium A tiled pool in the center of the **atrium**. It caught rainwater from the roof and channeled it to a **cistern.**

Import To buy or bring in goods from a foreign country.

Insula Literally translated means island, used to describe a block of buildings.

Lararium The family shrine. Usually a wooden cabinet with a shelf on which gifts were placed for the household gods.

Lava Molten rock.

Legionary A Roman soldier.

Magma A mixture of molten rock and gas.

Pumice stone A light, porous rock produced during volcanic eruptions.

Relief (In sculpture.) A carving where figures and objects project from a flat background.

Slave A person who is legally owned by another and has no freedom of action or right to property.

INDEX

ACKNOWLEDGMENTS

The extract on page 19 is taken from *The Letters of the Younger Pliny* translated by Betty Radice, (Penguin, 1963, 1969) page 172.

The cover illustration is by Angus McBride, the illustration on page 11 is by Malcolm S. Walker.

The publishers would like to thank the following for providing the photographs in this book: Mary Evans Picture Library 18, 26; Geoscience Features Picture Library 22(b), 23, 29; Werner Forman Archive 13, 19, 27; Ronald Sheridan Ancient Art and Architecture Collection 14, 18; Zefa 21, 22(t), 28.